UPDOG

IN THE SPOTLIGHT

OLIVIA RODRIGO

HIT SINGER-SONGWRITER

Heather E. Schwartz

Lerner Publications ◆ Minneapolis

Lerner Publications Company
An imprint of Lerner Publishing Group, Inc.
241 First Avenue North
Minneapolis, MN 55401 USA

For reading levels and more information, look up this title at www.lernerbooks.com.

Main body text set in ITC Franklin Gothic Std.
Typeface provided by Adobe Systems.

Designer: Viet Chu

Library of Congress Cataloging-in-Publication Data

Names: Schwartz, Heather E., author.
Title: Olivia Rodrigo: hit singer-songwriter / Heather E. Schwartz.
Description: Minneapolis : Lerner Publications, 2023. | Series: In the spotlight (Updog books) | Includes bibliographical references and index. | Audience: Ages 8–11 | Audience: Grades 4–6 | Summary: "Olivia Rodrigo took the world by storm with her debut album. From starring in Disney Channel shows to writing her own songs, Rodrigo never fails to thrill her many fans!"—Provided by publisher.
Identifiers: LCCN 2021051612 (print) | LCCN 2021051613 (ebook) | ISBN 9781728458366 (library binding) | ISBN 9781728463674 (paperback) | ISBN 9781728461793 (ebook)
Subjects: LCSH: Rodrigo, Olivia—Juvenile literature. | Singers—United States—Biography—Juvenile literature. | LCGFT: Biographies.
Classification: LCC ML3930.R634 S25 2022 (print) | LCC ML3930.R634 (ebook) | DDC 782.42164092—dc23

LC record available at https://lccn.loc.gov/2021051612
LC ebook record available at https://lccn.loc.gov/2021051613

Manufactured in the United States of America
1-50865-50202-3/17/2022

TABLE OF CONTENTS

A Songwriter Is Born

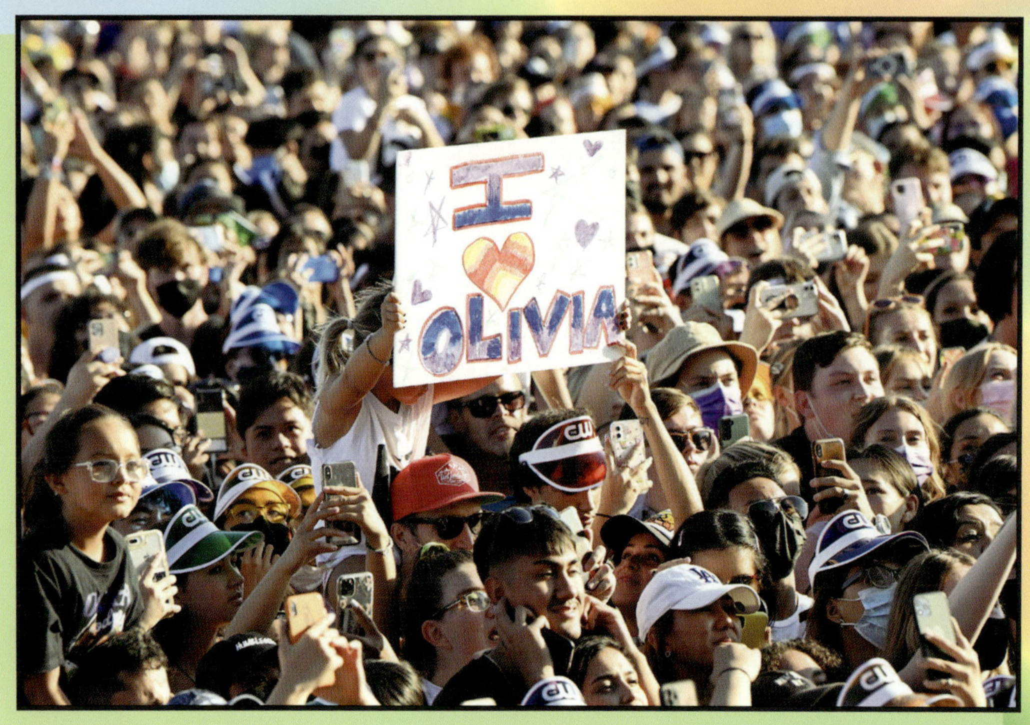

In 2021, the crowd cheered as Olivia Rodrigo belted out her song "good 4 u."

She smashed her first performance at the MTV Video Music Awards.

Growing up, she took singing lessons.

She acted in school plays.
She also learned to play piano.

UP NEXT!

Leveling up.

Working Her Talents

At twelve, she got a part on the show *Bizaardvark.*

Olivia learned guitar for the role.

Next, she starred in *High School Musical: The Musical: The Series.*

High School Musical's creators asked her to write a song for the show.

STAR STATS

Full name: Olivia Isabel Rodrigo

Date of birth: February 20, 2003

Hometown: Temecula, California

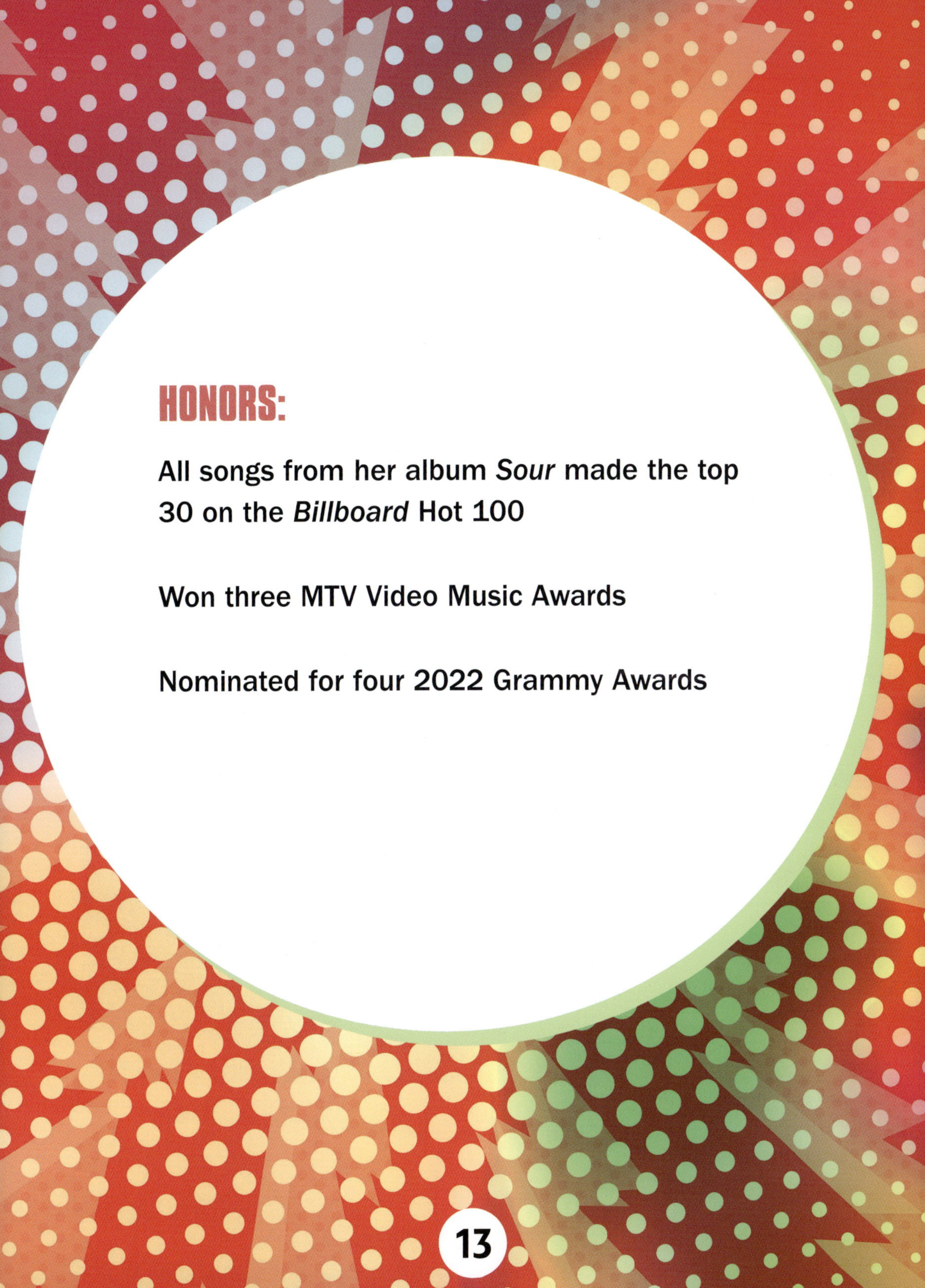

HONORS:

All songs from her album *Sour* made the top 30 on the *Billboard* Hot 100

Won three MTV Video Music Awards

Nominated for four 2022 Grammy Awards

Olivia wrote "All I Want." It was her first published song.

She landed a record deal.

She worked with a professional songwriter.

UP NEXT!

Breakout artist.

professional: relating to a job that requires special education, training, or skill

Top Pop Star

In 2021, Rodrigo released her first single, "drivers license."

single: one song

She released her debut album.

debut: first

It quickly hit No. 1 on the *Billboard* 200 albums chart.

Rodrigo wants to make more music.

Just like Olivia

Learning about music helped Rodrigo reach her goals. What's your goal? How could learning more help you reach it?

GLOSSARY

debut: first

professional: relating to a job that requires special education, training, or skill

single: one song

CHECK IT OUT!

IMDb: Olivia Rodrigo
https://www.imdb.com/name/nm7111120/

Kiddle: Olivia Rodrigo
https://kids.kiddle.co/Olivia_Rodrigo

Leigh, Anna. *Write and Record Your Own Songs*. Minneapolis: Lerner Publications, 2018.

Olivia Rodrigo Official Site
https://www.oliviarodrigo.com

Rossiter, Brienna. *Great Careers in Music*. Lake Elmo, MN: Focus Readers, 2022.

Schwartz, Heather E. *Zendaya: Hollywood Superstar*. Minneapolis: Lerner Publications, 2023.

INDEX

PHOTO ACKNOWLEDGMENTS

Image credits: Denise Truscello/Getty Images, p. 4; Kevin Mazur/MTV VMAs 2021/Getty Images, pp. 5, 18, 19; Jon Kopaloff/Teen Vogue/Getty Images, p. 6; Denise Truscello/iHeartMedia/Getty Images, p. 7; Matthew Simmons/Getty Images, p. 8; Kevin Winter/Getty Images, p. 9; AP Photo/GDA, p. 10; Jenny Anderson/Getty Images, p. 11; Theo Wargo/Getty Images, p. 12; AP Photo/Amy Harris/Invision, pp. 14, 17; Mat Hayward/iHeartRadio/Getty Images, p. 15; imtmphoto/Shutterstock.com, p. 16; Dave J Hogan/Getty Images, p. 20.

Cover image: Theo Wargo/Getty Images.